I0006417

Dental Informatics

Gurpreet Kaur
Parvinder Singh Baweja

Dental Informatics

Improving dental research,practice and education

LAP LAMBERT Academic Publishing

Imprint

Any brand names and product names mentioned in this book are subject to trademark, brand or patent protection and are trademarks or registered trademarks of their respective holders. The use of brand names, product names, common names, trade names, product descriptions etc. even without a particular marking in this work is in no way to be construed to mean that such names may be regarded as unrestricted in respect of trademark and brand protection legislation and could thus be used by anyone.

Cover image: www.ingimage.com

Publisher:
LAP LAMBERT Academic Publishing
is a trademark of
International Book Market Service Ltd., member of OmniScriptum Publishing Group
17 Meldrum Street, Beau Bassin 71504, Mauritius

ISBN: 978-3-659-48331-8

Copyright © Gurpreet Kaur, Parvinder Singh Baweja
Copyright © 2013 International Book Market Service Ltd., member of OmniScriptum Publishing Group

ACKNOWLEDGEMENT

At the very onset, I offer my deepest gratitude, profound thanks and humble offerings to the *Almighty* to whom I bow my head in reverence and with whose gracious and plentiful blessings this work was successfully completed.

It is my privilege to express my heartfelt gratitude and indebtedness to my teachers Dr. Kavipal Singh, Professor and Dr Kamleshwar Kaur, Reader, Department of Prosthodontics, Sri Guru Ram Das Institute of Dental Sciences and Research, Amritsar, for their guidance and support.

Words are inadequate to express my deep sense of gratitude to my family whose innumerable sacrifices, constant encouragement, advice and blessings are instrumental in my every accomplishment in life.

I am grateful to all my friends and well-wishers for rendering their co-operation.

Dr. GURPREET KAUR

This work is dedicated to

my sweet Daughter

Ustat

TABLE OF CONTENTS

DENTAL INFORMATICS

INTRODUCTION

Dental informatics is a young scientific discipline that is undergoing continual maturation. Eisner defined dental informatics as the "application of computer and information science to improve dental practice, research and program administration."[16]

Dental informatics has developed significantly since 1960s, when the first uses of informatics approaches to address dental issues were documented. The term 'dental informatics' was first used in a MEDLINE-indexed publication in 1986.It is represented by working groups such as American Medical Information Association and the American Dental Education Association.

Currently, two dental informatics training programs are in operation-Columbia University, 2000 and University of Pittsburgh, 2000; and the number of formally trained dental informaticians is slowly increasing.[47]

At the dawn of a new millennium, computers are appearing as an essential instrument alongside the handpiece in the dental operatory. They facilitate appointment scheduling and transaction posting, and have become the new center for dental office information technology—the nerve center for digital radiograph imaging, charting, and digital and photographic record keeping.[45]

Clinical dentistry has seen many informatics and information technology innovations, such as Florida probe, Oral CDX (a computer-assisted, brush biopsy test for the detection of oral cancer), computer based shade matching, and CEREC (a modular computer-aided design/ manufacturing system for creating ceramic restorations).[46]

The next stage in the development and expansion of this technology for the dental office is technology integration, which will allow the dentist to seamlessly link practice management, voice charting, intraoral cameras, CAD-CAM, lasers, electronic digital imaging, video imaging, digital radiography, and so forth, into a single potent system for complete clinical and practice management.[45]

The objective of the Artificial Intelligent Dental Agents is the analysis of dental decision-making, the design of a computer-based decision support system, as well as the testing of the decision structure in interactions with dental experts, practicing dentists, and patients. For prosthetic dentistry, clinicians have been shown how to use individual patient findings to sketch the possible treatment alternatives and later derive guidelines for the treatment. The planning module for fixed prostheses has already been integrated into a software agent.[16]

Adaptive hypermedia is a learner-centered approach first which evaluates the user's abilities and determines the individual learning style to structure and tailor the curriculum most efficiently.[53]

The application of dental informatics to oral genomics can aid in the molecular understanding of the genes and proteins that are responsible for the development and progression of oral diseases and disorders.[3]

The purpose of informatics is to solve practical problems for researchers, practitioners and education.

With a better understanding of its goals and methods, individuals in applied areas will be able to identify more easily how informatics could potentially help them in their own work.[1]

New techniques and technologies will facilitate the development of truly monumental applications, such as a comprehensive electronic oral health record, an automated dental treatment planning system for all diagnoses, or a system to profile patient risk for chronic oral diseases.[51]

That will be the era of Dental Informatics evolved!

As Jamei Paolinetti aptly puts it:

"Limitations live only in our minds. But if we use our imaginations, our possibilities become limitless. "

REVIEW OF LITERATURE

Pieper K, Klar R, Kessler P [37] **(1981)** described the use of microcomputer for recording dental epidemiologic data. The variability in epidemiologic studies can be reduced by standardizing the diagnostics criteria and recording methods. A portable data recording system that works on the basis of a microcomputer was developed. It consisted of the recording and transfer program, both written in programming language "BASIC". It enabled the examiner to record dental epidemiologic data with microcomputer in a dialog system under field conditions for dental caries. A mask screen was chosen so that the teeth are projected onto the screen with all surfaces. During input, checks could be carried out to detect illogical and contradictory entries. A visual and an acoustic signal indicated an error for which immediate correction can be made. The data were temporarily stored on disks. Subsequent to the completion of investigation they were automatically transmitted by a transfer program to the computer-system in the computer center which excluded any human errors occurring in the course of transfer of data. Advantages of microcomputer method over conventional system for recording dental epidemiologic data include: detection of dentist's errors during examination, less time for data collection, entry and transmission and fewer errors.

Wastell DG, Lilley JD [58] **(1988)** described computer system which ran successfully for several years in the Department of Conservative Dentistry at Manchester University. The dental educator confronts increasing demands for technically demanding training against a background of factors working to reduce the clinical experience of students: less dental disease, new educational emphases and greater cost-consciousness .The system   allowed the department to make more accurate and timely assessments of student progress. Training requirements were numerically defined: the system tallies the amount of work done by each student in a series of nine restorative techniques. The basic unit of information stored by the system was a computerized 'patient record'. The system was interactive and the displays provided the means whereby patient and student data are input, checked and updated. Data were automatically checked at input; hospital numbers checked for uniqueness and range checks for all items. The main document produced by the computer system was a summary of individual student progress: Plastics, Inlays/Crowns and Roots, together with an overall grading. This document was produced each month for the departmental board meeting. Low performance could be readily detected at an early preventive stage and counseling initiated. On the other hand, 'good' students could be signed off early in order to conserve resources. This reduced clinical costs and gave more opportunities to the slower candidates to meet their targets. It also enabled rapid and formal identification of students demonstrably ready and able to undertake more advanced work. A number of new applications of the system are under evaluation which included computation of the amount of outstanding work for each patient and cross-referrals.

Spohn E, Hardison D [54] **(1990)** discussed about the consortium to develop applications of information technology for the discipline of operative dentistry. The Interactive Videodisc (IVD) program entitled "DentfoWindow" was planned in the second meeting of the consortium in October 1987.It is designed to present information about the what, why, and how of IVD technology using dental educational images and examples. IVD allows the teacher to develop highly interactive, self-instructional computer assisted programs which can incorporate instant access to thousands of full color slide-type images, full- motion video, up to four channels of sound, all from a laser disc. Also developed was the program "Anatomic Features of the Permanent Dentition", which had five basic elements: brief tutorial, a pretest, instructional set to introduce the subject matter, program content and a post test. The four areas focused were surfaces, proximal spaces, divisions and external features. Next was the development of Audio Visual Connection (AVC) program which allowed digitization of still images from various video sources and capturing audio sources as computer file. This allowed the introduction of highly interactive audiovisual training materials using computer equipment. The Podium for AVC would be explored as flexible tool to develop simultaneously classroom and individualized presentations of a given body of material. It is hoped that this technology would allow rapid, inexpensive update of teaching materials that change frequently over time.

Abbey LM [2] **(1991)** attended the conference "Current Topics in Medical Informatics: Strategies and Architectures for Medical Application Development to foster Modularization, Sharing, and Integration", whose purpose was to identify priorities for the next decade of medical informatics. The meeting emphasized cooperation, sharing, interchange, and development of more comprehensive and useful applications. Informatics is rapidly becoming an accepted term in dentistry with American Association of Dental Schools in the lead. A clear administrative direction and support, dissemination of knowledge and sharing of knowledge have been the strong recommendations made in the conference. Sections with common needs for technology and data manipulation should seek each other out for collaborative work in developing new generic products with broad applicability. Three major impediments to sharing are innate personal reluctance, lack of standards for development, transfer and design of databases and data and the lack of clearly defined evaluation/peer review mechanism for educational and research software development. We must be familiar with changing technology so that we can participate wisely and productively in our future as it evolves.

Corry AM [11]**(2001)** reviewed the University of Missouri-Kansas City (UMKC) School of Dentistry Library outreach service database from 1988-1998 to determine the total number of contacts for all services, numbers of contacts for each service, overall number of items sent and the number of dental

7

health professionals contacting the services. The outreach services included the Dental Reference Service (DRS), the Career Opportunity Centre (COC) and the Instructional Resources Library (IRL).The author found that the Career Opportunity Centre received 55 percent of contacts for the years 1988-1998, while the Dental Reference Service received 26 percent of the total contacts and the Instructional Resources Library service received 19 percent. The Dental Reference Service contacts included reference inquiries, requests for searches, Loansome Doc requests and book circulation. It appears that University of Missouri-Kansas City School of Dentistry alumni are active information-seekers. Whether geographic accessibility or the professional statuses are factors determining information-seeking remains to be answered. These indicate that additional research should be done in the area of dental informatics. Information seeking behaviors are an important part of the active clinical practice and may become more important as evidenced-based dentistry becomes more prevalent.

Schleyer TK et al [43] **(2001)** conducted a measurement study to validate a preliminary survey for dental students as no validated survey instrument exists to measure dental students' use of, knowledge about, and attitudes towards computers. Several studies have surveyed students about their knowledge and opinions regarding computers, but none of them has established the reliability and validity of the instrument(s) used. The preliminary instrument contained five scales: computer use, information resource use, computer knowledge, capabilities of computer systems, and effects of computers on dental practice. Selected variables were summarized descriptively, and a factor analysis for each scale was performed. In addition, construct validity was assessed through co-relational analyses among several variables. Three hundred seventy surveys distributed to students at nine dental schools generated 156 responses (42 percent response rate). Sixty-four percent of respondents were male, 36 percent female. Respondents used computers an average approximately four hours per week, and most had begun using computers in 1991. All survey scales except computer use were one-dimensional. Computer use required a two-factor solution that distinguished between clinical and nonclinical uses of computers. The instrument can be used for a demonstration study, but should be continuously refined and validated.

Atkinson et al [5] **(2002)** discussed the deficiencies of electronic patient records for dental school clinics. The Electronic Patient Record (EPR) or computer based medical record is defined by the Patient Record Institute as 'A repository for patient information with one health-care enterprise that is supported by digital computer input and integrated with other information sources .'The information technology revolution coupled with everyday use of computers in clinical dentistry has created new demand for electronic patient records. Ultimately, the EPR should improve health care quality. The major short-term disadvantage is cost, including software equipment, training and personnel time involved in the associated business process re-engineering. An internal review committee with expertise in information technology and/or database management evaluated commercially available software in light of the unique needs of academic dental facilities. The primary concerns of most available software systems are procedure treatment planning, documentation of completed procedures, financial transactions and scheduling. Most systems lack scalability-that is, there is no enterprise version capable of supporting an entire dental school. The systems were deficient in security and privacy in a dental school environment, medical and dental history, a coding system for dental diagnoses, examination results, radiographic interpretation, treatment planning and education and quality assurance. The dental profession should develop a more common record with standard diagnostic codes and clinical outcome measures to make the EPR more useful for clinical research and improve the quality of care.

Actis LA et al[3] (2003) discussed the genetic and molecular characterization of Actinobacillusactinomycetemcomitans which causes periodontics and has multifactorial process pathogenesis. Much remains to be done to understand, in detail, the bacterial factors and host-pathogen interactions involved in the pathogenesis. Classic research approaches have provided a rather narrow picture of the cellular process. In contrast, a much wider picture could be obtained with the application of tools such as bioinformatics and genomics. These tools will provide global information regarding the differential expression of genes encoding factors and processes that lead to the pathogenesis of this disease. The genome of the clinical isolate HK1651has been completely sequenced and is in the final stages of annotation process. The genome size of this strain is 2,105,503bp and contains 2345 predicted open reading frames. About half of the genes of this dental pathogen encode proteins that were either classified as hypothetical, unclassified or of unknown function.PCR amplification of genomic DNA isolated from other A.Actinomycetemcomitans strains proved that **afe** and **afu** genes which code for periplasmic-binding protein-dependent transport (PBT) systems are present in all strains tested . Comparative genomics has the potential of helping us to understand the emergence and evolution of this human pathogen.

 The scientific community is already benefiting from bacterial genomes that have been completed and published, like that of S. mutansUA159, which is providing basic global information such as that related to gene composition, the presence of genetic elements potentially involved in genome evolution, and the mechanisms and elements involved in horizontal gene transfer. Certainly, this genomic information will be used to construct DNA microarrays (DNA chips) containing probes for each open reading frame found in the genome of this bacterium. Hybridization of these chips should provide data regarding the genetic components that are common and unique among them, information that should give insights into the genetic variations among bacteria without the burden of sequencing the entire genome of a large number of clinical isolates. Hybridization of DNA chips with labeled cDNA probes generated from RNA samples could be used to study differential gene expression and understand the host-pathogen interactions at the molecular level. Hence the genome – wide approach should provide a more complete picture of pathogenesis process of the diseases, and will facilitate the development of efficient diagnostic, preventive, and therapeutic measures.

Anusavice KJ [4] **(2003)** described informatics systems to assess and apply clinical research on dental restorative materials. Dental biomaterials are used clinically to restore function, to enhance esthetics, and to prevent or arrest demineralization of tooth structure. Studies of the clinical performance of restorations and prostheses made from these materials have generally focused on quality assessment and survival statistics. Data from these studies should provide probabilities of specific treatment outcomes that are useful for practicing dentists. However, the utility of these data is limited by the lack of national and international standards for assessing these clinical outcomes. Standardized approaches toward clinical informatics and treatment-decision analysis are urgently needed to minimize the variability of clinical outcomes reported in publications associated with direct and indirect restorative materials used for dental restorations and prostheses. A secondary set of inclusion and exclusion criteria must be formulated to answer specific questions in addition to evidence-based reviews of clinical performance. Establishing a national center as a clearinghouse for experimental designs and for storage of clinical research databases should ensure the accessibility of more consistent studies that are appropriate for inclusion in subsequent systematic reviews. In addition, much greater emphasis should be placed on courses in dental schools that provide instruction on clinical study design to enhance transfer of this information to clinical practices.

Bailit HL [6] **(2003)** discussed the challenges researchers face in accessing information on the dental delivery system, since this is the primary interface between dental HSR and informatics. According to Agency for Healthcare research and Quality (AHRQ): "Health Services Research examines how people get access to health care, how much care costs, and what happens to patients as a result of this care. The main goals of health services research are to identify the most effective ways to organize, manage, finance, and deliver high-quality care; reduce medical errors; and improve patient safety". The major barriers to the collection of primary population-based dental services data are lack of use of standard record systems by dentists, few dentists use electronic records and cost to abstract paper dental records being high. Because of the substantial costs associated with collecting primary data on dental services, charges, oral health status, etc., most dental HSR projects use secondary datasets. The value of secondary data from paid insurance claims is limited, because dentists code only services delivered and not diagnoses, and it is difficult to obtain and merge claims from multiple insurance carriers. A more recent social barrier is the demands on researchers made by the Health

Information Portability and Accountability Act (HIPAA). The implementation of this 1996 legislation requires researchers to have explicit permission from patients to access any patient-related information available in dental offices, hospitals, etc.

In a national demonstration project on the impact of community-based dental education programs on the care provided to underserved populations, a simplified dental visit encounter system has been developed. Senior students and residents from 15 dental schools (approximately 200 to 300 community delivery sites) will use computers or scannable paper forms to collect basic patient demographic and service data on several hundred thousand patient visits. Within the next few years, more dentists will use electronic records. To be of value to researchers, these data need to be collected according to a standardized record format and to be available regionally from public or private insurers. The "Pipeline" demonstration program has developed a simple system for collecting encounter data on thousands of patients receiving care in hundreds of delivery sites. This is an opportunity for dental health services and informatics researchers to gain invaluable experience on the organization and operation of a large-scale, patient-level data collection system.

Barath VS et al[7] **(2003)** conducted a study analyzing , two All-Ceramic (AC) materials—Empress 2 (EMP) and In-Ceram ALUMINA (ICA), along with the effects of 3 luting agents—viz. Zinc Phosphate cement, Glass Ionomer Cement (GIC), and Compolute (COMP),on the final color, using the CIELab system. It has been suggested that color training for dentists should be a part of the course in prosthetic dentistry. The CIELab color system (Commission Internationale de l'Éclairage) system facilitates color space presentation. Color differences (DeltaL, Deltaa, Deltab, and DeltaE) were calculated for samples with luting agents and for samples without luting agents with standard white and black backgrounds, with the use of a spectrophotometer, Luci 100 (Dr. Lange, Berlin, Germany). Darker ceramics showed less color variation. Luting agents altered the final color of the restoration. Zinc phosphate was least translucent, followed by Glass ionomer cement and Compolute. Marginal increases in thicknesses of In-Ceram ALUMINA samples (0.4 mm) do not show a statistically significant color difference. No method exists to predict the outcome of an all ceramic restoration based on consideration of the luting agent and the background color. A database with the color properties of the materials will be developed, along with an algorithm for calculation of color properties of dental restorative materials and final color predictions with various combinations and various background colors. The main purpose of this would be to eliminate traditional color matching and color prescription, thereby eliminating errors in human eye-color matching and prescription.

Bartling WC et al[8] **(2003)** described retrieval and classification of dental research articles. The information that researchers use in their scientific activities can come from many sources, such as the published literature, web sites, and databases. Successful retrieval of a corpus of literature on a broad topic can be difficult. In MEDLINE, the key words are known as the Medical Subject Headings (MeSH). The MeSHare a hierarchical system of words and phrases that are assigned to documents by human indexers to describe content and other related information such as study methodology. Terms were chosen with the goal of higher recall, or sensitivity. OVID (OVID technologies) interface was used to search the MEDLINE database- the English-language abstracts published between 1966 and 2002. Sixteen dental research experts categorized these articles, reading only the title and abstract, as either dental research, dental non-research, non-dental, or not sure. Identify Patient Sets (IPS), a probabilistic text classifier, created models, based on the presence or absence of words or Unified Medical Language System (UMLS) phrases that distinguished dental research articles from all others. These models were applied to a test set with different inputs for each article: title and abstract only, MeSH terms only, or both. MeSH term inclusion decreased performance. Computer programs that use text input to categorize articles may aid in retrieval of a broad corpus of literature better than indexing terms or key words alone. Upon successful retrieval of this literature, visual representation and statistical analysis may be used to examine trends and topics in dental and craniofacial research.

Chen JW et al [10] **(2003)** discussed teledentistry and its use in dental education. Teledentistry is a relatively new field that combines telecommunication technology and dental care. The initial concept of teledentistry developed as part of the blueprint for dental informatics which was drafted at a 1989 conference funded by the Westinghouse Electronics Systems Group in Baltimore. The term "teledentistry" was used in 1997, when Cook defined it as "the practice of using video-conferencing technologies to diagnose and provide advice about treatment over a distance. Teledentistry in education can be divided into two main categories: self-instruction and interactive videoconferencing. The advantage of interactive videoconferencing is that the user can receive immediate feedback. Both of these methods have been used in several studies and countries. The type of network connectivity used greatly affects the feasibility of teledentistry education. The cornerstones of modern teledentistry are the deployment of the Internet and broadband high-speed connections, which have helped teledentistry enter a new era. According to U.S. Army's experience orthodontics and periodontics are especially well-suited to teledentistry because much of the hands-on care can be rendered by dental assistants and hygienists. Dental radiology and imaging is another specialty area that is well-suited to teledentistry in education. Teledentistry can extend care to underserved patient populations, such as those in rural areas, at a reasonable cost. Some barriers still exist for teledentistry practice, including legal, educational and insurance issues. Most important, an experienced instructor is required for designing protocols, instructing students and providing necessary technical support. With thorough planning, however, teledentistry has a bright future.

Eplee H [15] **(2003)** described electronic management systems. The international development and deployment of an electronic modularized dental curriculum is central to the development of an electronic engine to be used for the effective management of dental education. This will ensure continuity in high quality of care across all boundaries, through the continuous updating of its content and linkages to contemporary resources and databases.

An electronic engine to be used for the effective management of dental education in a comprehensive dental school/hospital setting is at the core of an international 'virtual' dental education institution. The issue of policy development necessary to ensure consistency, quality and management for an electronic engine is at the very centre of: systems management and system databases; records of students, patients and personnel; and financial records.

The use of information systems can assist in improving the paper-based record in a number of ways as: elimination of illegibility, well addressed fragmentation of clinical data, efficient organization of the records, reduced level of missing records, information made available 24x7, regular update of medical history and summarized display of current health status of the patient.

Feldman et al proposed a framework design, referred to initially as the Computer-based Oral Health Record. The components of the design included Computerized Patient Record, Electronic Tools, Administrative Components, Financial Components and Educational Components. After examination the group suggested the following components for dental school management system: clinical systems; administrative system; educational systems; and research systems.

Finkeissen E et al [16] **(2003)** discussed about the web agents in treatment planning. The objective of the AIDA project (Artificial Intelligent Dental Agents, http://aida.uni-hd.de) is the analysis of dental decision-making, the design of a computer based decision support system, as well as the testing of the decision structure in interactions with dental experts, practicing dentists, and patients. The planning of the solution alternatives for an individual patient is based on a top-down structure for dental decision-making, aiming at a standardization of the argumentation. From a theoretical point of view, decision support can be provided only for anticipated decisions. Also, only parts of these anticipated decisions can be supported. Accordingly, a separation of these partial aspects has to take place before one is able to build decision support systems. For prosthetic dentistry, clinicians have been shown how to use individual patient findings to sketch the possible treatment alternatives and later derive guidelines for the treatment. The planning module for fixed prostheses has already been integrated into a software agent.

Gansky SA [19] **(2003)** compared the performance of logistic regression with KDD (Knowledge discovery and data mining) methods of CART (Classification and regression tree)and ANN

(Artificial neural network) in analyzing data from the Rochester caries study. Knowledge Discovery and Data Mining (KDD) have become popular buzzwords. But what exactly is data mining? What are its strengths and limitations? Classic regression, artificial neural network (ANN), and classification and regression tree (CART) models are common KDD tools. Some recent reports (e.g., Kattan et al., 1998) show that ANN and CART models can perform better than classic regression models: CART models excel at covariate interactions, while ANN models excel at nonlinear covariates. Model prediction performance is examined with the use of validation procedures and evaluating concordance, sensitivity, specificity, and likelihood ratio. To aid interpretation, various plots of predicted probabilities are utilized, such as lift charts, receiver operating characteristic curves, and cumulative captured-response plots. A dental caries study is used as an illustrative example. Informatics, in general, and dental informatics, in particular, are disciplines encompassing a variety of research areas, from molecular biology to library science to public health surveillance. Many dental informatics application areas utilize knowledge discovery and data mining (KDD)—semiautomatic pattern, association, anomaly, and statistically significant structure discovery in data. KDD operates at the intersection of artificial intelligence, machine language learning, computer science, engineering, and statistics. KDD has been named a Top Ten emerging technology that will change the world.

However, KDD is not alchemy—it does not turn lead into gold (i.e., bad data or flawed study designs into incredible, novel insights)—but rather KDD is a discipline using modern computing tools to solve problems.

Greenes RA [20] **(2003)** discussed decision support at the point of care. There has been a paradigm shift in clinical information systems. Formerly, the foci of development were the electronic medical record, information retrieval and reporting, scheduling, and various communications functions, as well as financial and billing applications. Over the past decade or so, however, emphasis has shifted increasingly to cost-effectiveness, error prevention, safety, and improvement of health care quality. This has required a new emphasis on incorporating executable knowledge and point-of-care decision support into clinical systems. Many applications in a clinical information system can benefit from the incorporation of medical knowledge to provide patient-specific, point-of-care decision support. These include computer-based provider order entry, referral, clinical result interpretation, consultation, adverse event monitoring, scheduling, shared patient-doctor decision-making, and generation of alerts and reminders, among others. To be executable, knowledge must be represented in the form of rules, constraints, calculations, guidelines, and other logical/algorithmic formats. The main difficulty is that the integration of such knowledge into clinical applications, when it occurs, tends to be very system- and application-specific, often encoded in a programming language, or even in the formatting specifications of a user interaction display. The data references invoked are highly dependent on the system/platform and electronic medical record implementation thus making it difficult and time-consuming to encode authoritative evidence-based knowledge, severely limits the ability to disseminate and share successes, and hampers efforts to review and update the logic as medical knowledge changes. Development of standards-based representations for medical knowledge, and tools for authoring/editing, dissemination, adaptation to local environments, and execution offer solutions to the problem.

Hammond P et al [22] **(2003)** described in a paper how biological and clinical problems stimulate research in biomedical informatics and how such research contributes to their solution. The computational models described use techniques from Logic Programming, Machine Learning, Computer Vision, and Biomathematics. They address problems in the development, growth, and repair of oral and craniofacial tissues arising in cell biology, clinical genetics, and dentistry. At the micro-level, the dynamic interaction of cells in the oral epithelium is modeled. A simulation model of the normal equilibrium state of epithelial cell production is being built so that it can subsequently be perturbed to simulate abnormal behavior. Currently, the model successfully reproduces aspects of epithelial cell behavior. At the macro-level, models are constructed of either the craniofacial shape of an individual or the craniofacial shape differences within and between healthy and congenitally abnormal populations. Point Distribution Model is generated to determine the variation in arch width and differences between triangular and square arches. With 3-D images of the soft tissues of the face, using 3-D photogrammetry, many new applications like standard anthropometric analyses can be performed on soft tissues by identifying anatomical landmarks.

One immediate application of a dense surface model of face shape is in tracking soft-tissue changes accompanying orthognathic surgery. Average faces can be computed for any set of faces. Using comparative studies it is useful to be able to discriminate between individuals with a syndrome and controls.

In between, in terms of scale, there are models of normal dentition and the use of computerized expert knowledge to guide the design of dental prostheses used to restore function in partially edentulous patients. RaPiD, a computer-aided design (CAD) tool has been developed to guide dentists to more acceptable designs. It generates descriptions of the RPD components as Horn clauses in a logic database defining which teeth are absent/present, those to be replaced by artificial teeth; which teeth have rests on them, and which have clasps to retain the prosthesis in the mouth.

Kirshner M [26] **(2003)** discussed the role of dental informatics research vis-à-vis the doctor-patient relationship and explores how it may inform the next generation of information technologies used in dental practice.

A high-value doctor-patient relationship is based on a set of parameters which include the interpersonal relationship between the patient and the doctor. Based on the Primary Care Assessment Survey model, measures of the interpersonal relationship are associated with communication, interpersonal care, contextual knowledge of the patient, and trust. Despite the proven value of the doctor patient relationship, current trends indicate that the quality of these relationships is on the decline due to rise of consumerism, decreased professionalization and organizational structure of health care delivery system. The advent of communication and information technologies has greatly affected the way in which health care is delivered and the relationship between doctors and patients. Its convergence with biomedical informatics offers an opportunity to affect the character of the doctor-patient relationship positively. Email communication as in providing patients with direct access to their own personal dental health records can enhance the dentist-patient relationship. Relevant information about the dentist and practice philosophy and policies on the internet makes a prospective patient determine whether his/her own values and preferences fit with those of the dentist. Non-Internet clinical applications include a wide range of devices and software programs that include: an electronic oral health record (EOHR), digital imaging; diagnostic applications; and decision support applications; the electronic oral health record being the centerpiece of information. Digital imaging, due to its immediacy and ease of understanding through recognizable visualizations affects the relationship. Others such as diagnostic, treatment planning, and decision support applications can also support a positive dentist-patient relationship. The communication and information technology application affected by model formulation are the electronic oral health record and personal health record; by system development research- electronic oral health record, teledentistry, treatment planners, decision support, and practice administration; by system installation research -human computer interface; and by study of effects research- the processes and outcomes resulting from its use. Overall, informatics research should provide insight that will inform the design and deployment of the next generation of communication and information technology used in dental practice—applications that will be explicitly designed to facilitate an enduring and trusting dentist-patient relationship.

Koch S [27] **(2003)** discussed a user centered system development approach based on extensive work analyses in interdisciplinary working groups, taking into account human cognitive performance. Special focus is put on analysis and design of the information and communication flow and on exploration of intuitive visualization and interaction techniques for clinical information. Two different research projects have been described which cover information technology support for chairside work in dentistry and for home health care of elderly citizens.

ORQUEST provides dentists with a fully integrated clinical workstation with IT support for quality assurance and development in oral health care. Fully integrated into the dental treatment unit, the workstation includes a voice-activated, electronic clinical patient record, support with regard to assessment and improvement of the technical quality of radiographs and image- and rule-based decision support for interpretation of radiographs and for diagnosis and treatment of oral mucosal lesions. In addition, video-conferencing, including application-sharing facilities for expert consultation, and improved dentist-dental technician communication and interactive programs for patient education and retrospective evaluation are provided. Hardware integration into the dental unit is done in an ergonomically optimal way.

The Swedish research and development project "Technical support for Mobile Close Care" focuses on the development and evaluation of work-scenario-oriented support for enhanced home care of elderly citizens. The aim of the project is to provide a seamless and consistent information flow between and among different health-care providers. A thorough user needs and work analysis, describing the entire work process and the different information and communication flows, is necessary. Access is given to prioritized information in adequate format (PIF) through a virtual health record with different data views for the different user categories. The design of the graphic user interface is optimized with regard to the respective work situation, the context of use, and the technical device that is used.

Krishnaraju RK et al [29] **(2003)** discussed comparative genomics and structure prediction of dental matrix proteins. Non-collagenous matrix proteins secreted by the ameloblasts (amelogenin) and odontoblasts (osteocalcin) play important roles in the mineralization of enamel and dentin. Comparative genomics approaches were used to identify the functional domains and model the three-dimensional structure of amelogenin and osteocalcin, respectively. Human amelogenin (accession AAK77213) and osteocalcin (accession P02818) sequences were used as a reference to find the homologous sequences from other species in GenBank. Multiple sequence analysis of amelogenin in different species showed a high degree of sequence conservation at the nucleotide and protein levels. At the protein level, motifs (a sequence pattern that occurs repeatedly in a group of related proteins or genes), conserved domains, secondary structural characteristics, and functional sites of amelogenin from lower phyla were similar to those of the higher-level mammals, reflecting the high degree of sequence conservation during vertebrate evolution. Predicting the three-dimensional structures of protein from sequence data by comparative modeling provides much-needed information on which experiments can be planned. In a search for domains with known 3-D structure in the conserved domain database, human osteocalcin aligned with human coagulation factor VIIa and no structural template was found for human amelogenin. The corresponding osteocalcin domain

17

consists of 43 amino acids with glutamic acid residues which have been shown in the 3-D structure as high-affinity calcium-binding gamma glutamic acid residues. In addition, the domain has alpha helical structures similar to those of the template .The structure provides evidence that osteocalcin is possibly involved in mineralization in dental and bone structures by similar mechanisms.

Kuo WP [30] **(2003)** reviewed application of bioinformatics to oral genomics. The "informatics revolution" in both bioinformatics and dental informatics will eventually change the way we practice dentistry. This convergence will play a pivotal role in creating a bridge of opportunity by integrating scientific and clinical specialties to promote the advances in treatment, risk assessment, diagnosis, therapeutics, and oral health-care outcome. This application to dental medicine, termed "oral genomics", can aid in the molecular understanding of the genes and proteins, their interactions, pathways, and networks that are responsible for the development and progression of oral diseases and disorders. Challenging areas that can benefit from the large-scale genomic approach are oral squamous cell carcinoma (OSCC), craniofacial development and malformation, and autoimmune diseases. As the result of the Human Genome Project, new advances have prompted high-throughput technologies, such as DNA microarrays, which have become accepted tools in the biomedical research community. Oral squamous cell carcinoma is an aggressive epithelial malignancy which needs new prognostic and predictive factors for classification of different stages. There are subtle changes that occur in its progression that are not captured through histology reports. Expression profiling using microarrays can be a means to refine conventional and histopathological assessment of the samples, allowing for a more accurate prediction of disease course. It is anticipated that dental informatics and bioinformatics and the incorporation of clinical data into the analysis of genomic information will increase our understanding of the mechanisms underlying the biological challenges in dentistry .This new approach to dental medicine will be both molecularly informed and informatically empowered.

Rekow D [38] **(2003)** discussed the informatics challenges in tissue engineering and biomaterials. A fundamental issue that informatics could address for tissue engineering is to describe and to predict the cascade of biochemical and cellular reactions that occur as a function of time and implant material: surface texture, micro porosity; pore size, density, and connectivity; and three-dimensional configuration. Behavior of ceramics, a subset of tissue-engineering scaffold materials and a mainstay of dental restorations, has been studied extensively for very thin layers and for thicknesses greater than 2 mm. Until recently, little has been known about dentally relevant thickness of 1-2 mm. Performance of crowns is a complicated function of an array of variables. As with tissue engineering, much is known about individual factors. Little is known about interactions of those factors. It is easy to evaluate flat samples in a laboratory. It is far more complex and expensive to test real crowns on real teeth. The challenge to the informatics team is to add insight into approaches that can address where, in the continuum from flat-polished materials to 10-year clinical data, clinical performance can be accurately predicted. Informatics approaches and the inclusion of informaticians on multidisciplinary teams offer possibilities for new insight into approaches to address complicated, expansive problems. Both tissue engineering and biomaterials offer challenges in fundamental understanding of complex interactions that could benefit from this new insight.

Robinson MA [39] **(2003)** discussed the issues and strategies for faculty development in technology and biomedical informatics. Biomedical informatics and technology are becoming important components of dental education. The tools and techniques now available have the potential for significant impact on teaching and research by improving the way information is acquired, stored, retrieved, and managed. However, a gap exists between those who create, introduce, or implement the technology applications and the faculty in dental schools faced with the challenge of using it. The technology is only as effective as the faculty who use it. Once technology integration has taken place, faculty can perform evaluations and provide insights regarding improvements or development of additional technologies. For technology and informatics to thrive in the areas of didactic teaching, clinical teaching, and clinical practice, more than a select few must understand the potential applications. Policies regarding use of technology should be established to guide expectations of administrators, faculty, students, and staff. These include use of equipment and facilities, training, copyright and intellectual property knowledge, process for introducing/implementing new technologies or technology-based processes, and mechanism for technical support that provides clear instructions for what to do in the event of hardware or software failure. Once a decision is made as to what will be included in the faculty development program, other judgments need to be determined regarding the frequency, setting, level of participation required, selection of trainers, and mechanism for evaluation, feedback, and ongoing support.

Alternatives to faculty development programs include web-based training environments, convenience training, train-the-trainer approaches, and coaching programs. Web-based training is becoming a viable alternative that offers convenience and just-in- time training.

The intersection between pedagogy, technology, and informatics is becoming inevitable. As dental schools increasingly embrace technology and informatics, the need to address faculty development will intensify.

Considering the value and benefits of technology and informatics, dental schools must be willing to make the investment necessary to implement strategies that will improve chances for successful implementation.

Rosenberg H et al [40] **(2003)** performed a systematic review of the published literature comparing Computer-aided learning (CAL) with other teaching methods to assess the effectiveness of CAL programs in dental education. CAL, self-instructional programs provide an accessible, interactive, and flexible way of presenting curriculum material.

Articles formally assessed for inclusion met the criteria namely randomized controlled trials comparing CAL with any other method of instruction, and the use of academically homogeneous dental students or dental professionals with objective, predefined outcome criteria measuring performance, time spent, and attitudes. The searches located a total of 1,042 articles; of these, only twenty-seven articles met the inclusion criteria. Further, quality assessment identified twelve studies that were included in the final review. Five of the studies documented statistically significant differences in outcome measures (scores on multiple choice, written or oral tests, and clinical performance) favoring CAL over comparison group(s), while six revealed no statistically significant differences. One study documented a greater improvement in test scores in the seminar group over the CAL group. Participants' attitudes towards CAL in the included studies were also discussed. The study concluded that CAL is as effective as other methods of teaching and can be used as an adjunct to traditional education or as a means of self-instruction.

Schleyer TK, Johnson LA [41] **(2003)** discussed evaluation of educational software.Evaluation is an important component of developing educational software. Ideally, such evaluation quantifies andqualifies the effects of a new educational intervention on the learning process and outcomes. Conducting meaningful and rigorouseducational evaluation is difficult. Challenges in evaluating educational software include defining and measuring educational outcomes, accounting formedia effects, coping with practical problems in designing studies, and asking the right research questions. Practical considerations that make the design of evaluation studies difficult include confounding, potentially small effect sizes, contamination effects, and ethics. Two distinct approaches to evaluation are objectivist and subjectivist. These two complement each other in describing the whole range of effects a new educational program can have. Objectivist demonstration studies should be preceded by measurement studies that assess the reliability and validity of the evaluation instrument(s) used. Many evaluation studiescompare the performance of learners who are exposed to either the new program or a more traditional approach. However, this method is problematic because test or exam performance is often a weak indicator of competence and may fail to capture important nuances in outcomes. Subjectivist studies are more qualitative in nature and may provide insights complementary to those gained with objectivist studies. Educational software is here to stay, and evaluating its effectiveness is an important goal in advancing the state of the art in this field. It is being heavily invested on and such investments should be founded on a good understanding of real and expected effects. A progressively better understanding of what works and what does not will ultimately allow us to improve the outcomes, economics, and efficiency of learning.

Schleyer TK et al [42] **(2003)** described a well-equipped dental office. Information technology, or IT, applications for dental practice continues to develop rapidly. More than 85 percent of all dentists use computers in their offices, and the number of clinical uses for the computer is on the rise. This article discusses the state of the art of several technologies, provides an integrative view of a technologically well-equipped office and offers several guidelines for technology purchasing decisions.

Most administrative applications are relatively mature and are required for the smooth functioning of today's dental offices. Clinical applications—such as dental and medical histories, charting, digital imaging and treatment applications, and decision support—vary in their degree of maturity. Most Internet applications—such as Internet-based scheduling and e-mail communication with patients—still are an optional adjunct for dental practices. Practitioners should develop a comprehensive plan for implementing or updating the IT infrastructure in their offices. Issues to be considered in technology purchasing decisions include usability, integration, work flow support, cost-benefit analysis and compliance with standards.

Schleyer TK [47] **(2003)** described dental informatics as an emerging biomedical informatics discipline. Concurrent with the development of computer hardware, information science, computer science, and telecommunications evolved as the core research fields contributing to the computer revolution. From those early beginnings, medical problems and applications provided significant impetus and stimulus to the development of new principles in computer science and information science. In the 1960s, "informatics" emerged as a distinct concept. AlekseiMikhailov first defined the term as the discipline that "studies the structure and general properties of scientific information and the laws of all processes of scientific communication." The term "medical informatics" first appeared in France at the same time and made its entry into the English literature in 1974. Twelve years later, "dental informatics" was first used in a MEDLINE-indexed publication (Zimmerman et al., 1986).

Friedman has described the tower of science in biomedical informatics which presents model formulation at the lowest level, system development and installation as the next step and topped by study of effects. Dental informatics is a small but growing discipline. The description of biomedical informatics as a research discipline highlights both differences and areas of overlap with information technology (IT).

While informatics is primarily a research discipline aimed at uncovering fundamental principles and methods relating to information and computers, information technology is primarily focused on the implementation, application, and support of computer technology and telecommunications.

The scientific methods in informatics come primarily from four research areas: computer science, information science, cognitive science, and telecommunications. However, many other fields such as social sciences, psychology, anthropology, linguistics, engineering, and mathematics also contribute to the scientific basis of informatics.

Many innovations in computerizing medical records, however, have had little or no utility for dentistry. For instance, representational schemes and standards for clinical data, such as the SNOMED, the Reed Codes, the ICD, and HL- 7, typically don't represent dental concepts and data very well. Despite the fact that many practical problems require discipline-specific solutions, broad and interdisciplinary collaboration within the biomedical informatics community seems to be one of the best ways to develop these solutions.

Sebastiani P[50] **(2003)** outlined the opportunities and the challenges of machine learning research, and described where the efforts of "cracking the code of life" can most benefit from a Bayesian approach, and it identifies some potential applications of Bayesian machine learning methods to the genomic analysis of squamous cell carcinomas of the head and neck. With the completion of the Human Genome Project and the growing computational challenges presented by the large amount of genomic data available today, machine learning is becoming an integral part of biomedical research and plays a major role in the emerging fields of bioinformatics and computational biology. Bayesian methods provide a principled way to incorporate external information into the data analysis process. In a Bayesian approach, the data analysis process starts with a given probability distribution. The ability to integrate data with external information, a trademark of Bayesian analysis, provides a natural framework for integrating various forms of information available about the genome, and it has already been exploited to develop linkage models of complex diseases, such as autism. The presence of well-characterized structural abnormalities in Head and Neck Squamous Cell Carcinomas lends itself to an integrative genomic approach, Bayesian Methods, able to combine this structural information with functional data derived from microarray studies. Bayesian clustering methods can leverage on the combination of genomic and phenotypic information to understand the interplay between clinical outcomes and identify new classifications able to disambiguate the well known heterogeneity of disease.

Spallek H[53] **(2003)** described adaptive hypermedia. Traditional online dental education courses followthe broadcast paradigm which centers on the teacher, not thestudent. This one-size-fits-all approach resembles a mass productionidea which cannot take individual learnercharacteristics into account. Most online course designs do not address the issue that users with different goals and knowledge may be interested in different pieces of information about atopic. Adaptive hypermedia (AH) is an emerging field in education research which investigates how computer systems can overcome this problem. It can be applied to any course content. This learner-centered approach first considers the learning goal(s), then evaluates the user's abilities and determines the individual learning style, to structure and tailor the curriculum most efficiently. The presented adaptive hypermedia environment exploits various concepts of adaptive hypermedia. The system collects data to create a model of the individual user, which is continuously refined based on test results throughout the course. The system then adapts the learning material dynamically, using active and passive curriculum sequencing and adaptive presentation. However, online dental education faces many challenges-weak models for online learning, inability of static web pages to take into account individual learner characteristics, absence of single best instructional technique and lack of social and emotional relationship between instructor and learner.

Combined with sound application of usability engineering principles and the facilitation of peer-learner contacts as well as learner-instructor contacts, adaptive hypermedia could serve as a new paradigm for educational software.

Hendricson WD et al [23] **(2004)** conducted a study to evaluate electronic curriculum implementation at North American Dental Schools. Electronic curriculum, or E-curriculum, refers to computer-based learning including educational materials available on CD or DVD, online courses, electronic mechanisms to search the literature, email, and various applications of instructional technology including providing laptops to students, multimedia projection systems, and Internet-compatible classrooms. In spite of enthusiasm about the potential for E-curriculum to enhance dental education, there is minimal guidance in the literature to assist schools with implementation. The study objectives were: 1) identify U.S. and Canadian dental schools that have initiated mandatory laptop programs and assess cost, faculty development issues, extent of curricular use, problems, and qualitative perceptions; 2) determine the extent to which twenty-two other E-curriculum resources were available and used at North American dental schools; and 3) identify factors that influenced E-curriculum implementation. A twenty-six item questionnaire, known as the Electronic Curriculum Implementation Survey (ECIS), was mailed to all sixty-six North American dental schools (ten Canadian and fifty-six U.S. schools) during 2002-03 with a response rate of 100 percent. Twenty-five of the twenty-six ECIS questions employed a menu-driven, forced choice format, but respondents could provide amplifying comments. Fifty-three questionnaires were completed by associate deans for academic affairs, three by deans, and ten by instructional technology (IT) managers, IT committee chairs, or directors of dental informatics departments. The survey found that

E-curriculum implementation among North American dental schools is following the classic innovation pattern in which a few early adopting institutions proceed rapidly while the majority of potential adopters make modifications slowly. Fourteen U.S. dental schools have established mandatory laptop programs for students. Ten of these laptop programs were created in the past two years; respondents reported numerous growing pains but were generally pleased with their progress. Other E-curriculum capabilities were incorporated into courses more frequently at laptop schools than the fifty-two non-laptop schools including websites, online course evaluations, and instructor use of email to communicate with students. Few dental schools use online courses, and at most schools, few faculties have received training in online instructional techniques. Virtually all North American dental schools have provided substantial instructional technology resources to their faculty, but use of twenty-two components and capabilities of E-curriculum was limited, especially at schools without laptop programs. Various faculty-related issues were reported as implementation barriers including lack of time, skill, and incentive to develop educational software. It was concluded that many North American dental schools, especially those with laptop programs, are functioning at the "learn by doing" phase of initial implementation in a four-stage innovation adoption model. E-curriculum planners should pay close attention to implementation problems that occur at this stage where many innovation efforts break down.

Johnson LA [25] **(2004)** summarized the core of biomedical informatics curriculum (biomedical informatics knowledge, data management, and software engineering) for dental research. It also summarizes the obstacles that must be overcome for all dental research students to receive the training in biomedical informatics they require. Dental researchers collaborating closely with biomedical informaticians have achieved many advances in oral health research, such as in mapping human genetics and addressing oral health disparities. Advances will continue to increase as dental researchers and biomedical informaticians study each others' disciplines to increase the effectiveness of their collaborative research. The combined skills will greatly increase the effectiveness of dental research. These issues are: a lack of biomedical informatics faculty, a lack of biomedical informatics courses, and a lack of accreditation standards. Last, intra- and inter-institutional collaboration solutions are described. Dental education has three major issues to overcome prior to the routine implementation of biomedical informatics instruction in the education of dental researchers. These issues include a dearth of faculty with biomedical informatics expertise, lack of biomedical informatics courses appropriate for dental researchers and lack of accreditation standards. Due to a lack of faculty with expertise in informatics, dental education is currently unable to teach its dental research students biomedical informatics skills. Dentistry is similar to the other biomedical professions in this dilemma in its search for a solution. The key to current successful solutions is intra and inter-institutional collaboration. The informatics training programs at both Columbia

University and the University of Pittsburgh are examples of intra-institutional collaboration in which the dental school is a part of a broader health sciences graduate program in biomedical informatics. Biomedical informatics is changing the way dental research is being done. These changes are becoming so pervasive that dental researchers require a background in biomedical informatics. This instruction needs to be carefully planned to meet the needs of educational and clinical researchers as well as biomedical researchers. Instruction should include an overview of biomedical informatics, followed by the application of biomedical informatics in subsequent research courses. Dental educators need to join together and support those pioneers who are willing to try new approaches to biomedical informatics training. Only then will we create a dental research community in which biomedical informatics enables new knowledge to be efficiently and effectively generated and disseminated.

Mendonça EA [35] **(2004)** discussed the characteristics of clinical decision support systems, addressed the challenges in developing them, identified potential barriers for their use in clinical practice, and provided perspectives for the future.

Clinical decision-support systems (CDSSs) are computer programs that are designed to provide expert support for health professionals making clinical decisions. The goal of these systems is to help health professionals analyze patient data and make decisions regarding diagnosis, prevention, and treatment of health problems. CDSS applications may be standalone systems, or they may interact with other tools such as an electronic dental record, an order entry system, or a radiology system. They may deliver a recommendation for the patient's treatment and future evaluation as well. Radiology systems, for instance, may generate messages if a radiograph is taken too often or if a radiographic examination is due. Most CDSSs have four basic components: inference engine (IE), knowledge base (KB), explanation module, and working memory. The IE is the main part of any such system. The knowledge used by the IE is represented in the KB. The collection of patient data may be stored in a database or may exist in the form of a message. This collection is known as "working memory." Patient data may include demographics (i.e., date of birth, gender), allergies, medications in use, previous dental or medical problems, and other information. The last component, the explanation module, is not present in all CDSSs. This module is responsible for composing justifications for the conclusions drawn by the IE in applying the knowledge in the KB against patient data in the working memory. CDSSs can be classified as open- or closed loop systems. In an open-loop system, the CDSS draws the conclusions but takes no action directly of its own. An application that generates an alert or reminder is an example of such systems. The final decision on the action to be taken, if any, is made by the clinician. In the closed-loop system, the action can be implemented directly without the intervention of a human.

Spallek H et al [52] **(2004)** designed an anonymous survey of twenty-one questions in an effort to better understand what kinds of information sources the applicants at The University of Pittsburgh's School of Dental Medicine (SDM) , a medium-sized, private, state-related dental school, used to make their application decisions; which information they perceived as useful during each phase of the overall application process; how they ranked the school website compared to those of other dental schools that they considered; and what they thought could make the website better.As other schools had done recently, the SDM made a substantial effort to upgrade its website in 2003. Internal satisfactionand anecdotal data notwithstanding, there is no measure of the website's usefulness in attracting applicants.

The study supported the notion that applicants rely in part on dental school websites during the application process. Data from this study point to the areas that are of most interest to applicants when they visit a dental school website. This information could help dental school administrators determine the effort they should spend on their school's website as an advertising and recruitment tool. It is recommended that dental schools make the most important application-related information and criteria easy to find.

Flores-Mir C et al [17] **(2006)** conducted an anonymous, self-administered survey of Canadian dentists by Mail to determine the frequency of computers in Canadian dental offices and to assess their use; to evaluate Internet access and use in Canadian dental offices; and to compare use of computers and the Internet by Canadian dentists, by the general public and by other dental groups. A potential mailing list of 14,052 active Canadian dentists was compiled from the 2003 records of provincial regulatory bodies. For each province, 7.8% of the general dentists were randomly selected with the help of computer software. The surveys were mailed to this stratified random sample of 1,096 dentists. The response rate was 28%. The proportion of Canadian dentists in this sample who had in-office computers was 90%.Canadian dental offices are high consumers of Internet services .A high proportion of the Canadian dentists surveyed used computers in their offices, primarily for administrative tasks (accounting, bookkeeping and scheduling) rather than clinical tasks. Internet access was common and there is significant use of high-speed access among Canadian dentists. The main reasons for not having in-office Internet access included security and privacy concerns and lack of need for or interest in the service. Canadian dentists' Internet use was greater than that of American dentists, private enterprise, and the North American public in general.

Flores-Mir C et al [18] **(2006)** conductedan anonymous, self-administered survey of Canadian dentists by mail. A potential mailing list of 14,052 active Canadian dentists was compiled from the 2003 records of provincial regulatory bodies. For each province, 7.8% of the dentists were randomly selected with the help of computer software. The survey was undertaken to determine dentists' perceptions of the usefulness of digital technologies in improving dental practice and resolving practice issues; to determine dentists' willingness to use digital and electronic technologies; to determine perceived obstacles to the use of digital and electronic technologies in dental offices; and to determine dentists' attitudes toward Internet privacy issues. More than 60% of the dentists indicated that computer technology was quite capable or very capable of improving their current practice by increasing patient satisfaction, decreasing office expenses, increasing practice efficiency, increasing practice production, improving record quality and improving case diagnosis and treatment planning.

More than 50% of respondents reported that digital photography and digital radiography were quite useful or very useful. About 70% of the dentists agreed or strongly agreed with using digital and electronic technologies to consult with dental specialists. Cost of equipment and lack of comfort with technology were regarded as significant or insurmountable obstacles by substantial proportions of respondents. Finally, lack of face to-face communication, incompatible software or hardware, problems with scheduling for videoconferencing, and security or privacy issues were significant or insurmountable obstacles for less than 40% of the dentists. The respondents felt that digital and electronic technologies were useful for most aspects of dental practice. For certain aspects (increased sharing of patient information and reduction in duration of appointments) the perception of usefulness was lower, but about 40% of respondents still perceived the technologies as quite capable or very capable of improving practice.

These are related to broader issues of time management (and lack of personal time), patient cooperation and practice management, all of which relate to orthodontists' stress and personal satisfaction. It has been assumed that determinants of stress and personal satisfaction are similar among Canadian orthodontists and dentists.

Digital photography and digital radiology were considered more useful than electronic models, electronic referral forms and paperless charting. Dentists appear more open to communicating electronically with specialists than with patients. The major obstacles to the general use of these technologies were related to cost, lack of comfort with technology and differences in legislation between provinces and countries. Privacy issues were not perceived as a significant barrier.

Gwilliam JR et al [21] (2006) conducted a study which evaluated the reproducibility of 24 soft tissue landmarks on six three-dimensional (3D) facial scans. The reproducibility of facial landmarks has been studied at length in two dimensions through the role of cephalometrics in orthodontics. However, as the face is a three-dimensional (3D) structure, the need to record its position in three dimensions has been highlighted. The use of laser scans and stereophotogrammetry have gained most favour in the orthodontic literature, principally because they are both non-invasive and non-ionizing.

Stereophotogrammetry is a method of obtaining an image by means of one or more stereo pairs of photographs taken simultaneously.

For the intraoperator data, 12 of the 24 landmarks were found to be reproducible to within a 1 mm standard deviation for each plane of space. The interoperator data showed lower reproducibility with just two landmarks showing less than a 1 mm standard deviation in all three planes of space. Familiarity with three-dimensional facial scans and associated software programs is important in improving reproducibility. In addition, the landmarks investigated in this study included those not often used. It is suggested that landmarks showing poor reproducibility for both inter- and intraoperator data should be avoided, if at all possible, or at least used with caution.

McGrath C et al [34] (2006) undertook a project with an objective to adapt an interactive computer program to manage a problem-based dental curriculum. Through application of commercial database software- Curriculum Analysis Tools (CATs)-an electronic database for all modules of a five-year problem-based program was developed. This involved inputting basic information on each problem case relating to competencies covered, key words (learning objectives), participating faculty, independent study, and home-work assignments, as inputting information on contact hours. General reports were generated to provide an overview of the curriculum. In addition, competency, key word, manpower, and clock-hour reports at three levels (individual problem based learning course component, yearly, and the entire curriculum) were produced. Key word reports can be generated to display all key words relating to learning issues covered in one problem case. Competency reports provide information on where and what competencies were covered relating to each problem case. Clock hour analysis provide information about the actual time spent on a case, or spent yearly, or on the overall learning throughout the whole course. One of the most useful applications of the program is its ability to provide information on which specific learning topics have been addressed and to what depth at specific times in the curriculum. The next phase in the application of an interactive computer program to manage a problem based learning dental curriculum should be to develop a strategy to link the outcomes to various components of the curriculum which can facilitate greater understanding of the link between the process and outcomes in dental education .

Boynton JR et al [9] (2007) undertook an exploratory study to determine students' assessment of portable digital video instruction (using the Apple® iPod®) and to compare examination performance among groups of predoctoral dental students who did and did not utilize portable digital video instruction as a supplement to a conventional pediatric behavior management lecture. The students received a one-hour lecture on communication with the parent and child patient as part of their regular sophomore pediatric dentistry curriculum. Digital audio and digital video versions of the lecture were made available to all 113 students and eleven student volunteers were loaned portable digital video players (the iPod) containing the lecture for a two-week period. Students who had used the iPod to review the digital video lecture material favored this medium as a pedagogical instrument and as a group performed significantly better on the examination than those who had not reviewed the digital material. It was concluded that the portable digital instructional videos may be a useful educational methodology to help predoctoral dental students acquire knowledge in pediatric behavior management.

Lacopino AM [31] **(2007)** described the influence of new science on dental education. According to him, advances in all aspects of science and discovery continue to occur at an exponential rate, leading to a wealth of new knowledge and technologies that have the potential to transform dental practice. This "new science" within the areas of cell/molecular biology, genetics, tissue engineering, nanotechnology, and informatics has been available for several years; however, the assimilation of this information into the dental curriculum has been slow. For the profession and the patients, it serves to benefit fully from modern science, new knowledge and technologies must be incorporated into the mainstream of dental education. Educational reforms at dental schools are based on addition of new curricular elements and include innovative approaches that introduce concepts regarding new advances in science, evidence-based foundations, and translational research. The Marquette University School of Dentistry restructured its curriculum. The first phase of the transition involved elimination of outdated or repetitive content; reduction of traditional lecture-based, discipline-specific courses; integration of basic biomedical, behavioral, and clinical sciences content into appropriately sequenced four-year educational tracks; implementation of case-based rounds and facilitated discussions using clinical and biomedical correlates for continuous reinforcement of key concepts; and establishment of early clinical experiences and community based experiential learning opportunities. The second phase of transition involved development of a dedicated curricular track record providing continuous exposure to new sciences concepts and applications and student research activity throughout all four years of dental education. Also, comprehensive faculty development initiatives were undertaken.

The University of Connecticut School of Dental Medicine developed a unique program element in "Biodontics" to introduce new science concepts related to translational research.

The University of Texas Health Science Center initiated curriculum redesign involving preparation of Critically Appraised Topic summaries that arise pertinent to patient care and the development of searchable online database of informative Critically Appraised Topics.

Oak MR [36] **(2007)** reviewed barriers to implementing health informatics in developing countries. Globalization of health informatics infrastructures is needed to have significant growth in improving quality and capacity of healthcare sector in developing countries. Right of universal access to information and communication services is new component of the UN's principles of human rights and development. At present the health information infrastructure remains inadequate to meet the needs of rising population.

Major problem is of financial constraints. Inadequate resources will affect the delivery of treatment and follow-up. An even bigger constraint on implementing effective healthcare practices is politics. Conflicts of interest with medical profession also value the freedom to practice Medicine. Culture and socio-ecological factors play important roles. Some cultures restrict access to the World Wide Web and in particular to certain medical illustrations of the human body, in some, information flow is more restricted for political purposes.

Population inflation and social crises in large proportion in the developing and underdeveloped world are creating fundamental barriers such as poverty and illiteracy. Enforcing the legislation is usually harder in developing countries as acceptance of transformation in any system is delayed in community development.

More challenging is the problem of convincing individuals to new technologies. Migration of content of health information from paper-based to a digital format is complicated for health workers. Lack of infrastructures, untrained personnel, and other conditions, impose strong limits to the introduction of new technologies. Addressing the special needs of the undeveloped countries would be the first step towards solving the problem. Commitment to good governance, development and poverty reduction, comprehensive dealing with the debt problems, program of debt relief and cancellation of official bilateral debt can enhance the progress. Resources should be invested primarily in safe and effective interventions. Strong communication infrastructure, information sharing, and continuous training of health professionals are pillars of health informatics. Standards will play a major role in the diffusion and interoperability of systems. To reduce the time and resources required in IT utilization important examples from developed countries can be followed.

Robust and affordable connectivity, particularly to rural areas in developing countries should be provided which can fully exploit the potential of handheld computers and wireless connectivity.

Telemedicine systems have some advantages but the lack of infrastructures, low income levels, and other conditions, impose strong limits to the introduction of new technologies.

Thyvalikakath TP et al [55] **(2007)** conducted a pilot study using heuristic evaluation (a method in which reviewers judge the user interface and system functionality as to whether they conform to established principles of usability and good design) to provide an initial description of potential usability problems in four major problem management systems- Dentrix, EagleSoft, SofDent and PracticeWorks. Heuristic evaluations to identify potential usability problems that may be encountered during the clinical care process were performed. Each researcher performed three common clinical documentation tasks on each problem management systems and examined the clinical user interface of each system using a published list of 10 software heuristics. An observer recorded all findings, summarized the results and totaled the heuristic violations across all programs. The authors found 229 heuristic violations. Consistency and Standards, Match Between System and the Real World, and Error Prevention were the heuristics that were violated most commonly. The patterns of heuristic violations across software packages were relatively similar. The findings provide an initial assessment of potential usability problems in four problem management systems. The identified violations highlight aspects of dental software that may present the most significant problems to users. Heuristic violations in problem management systems may result in usability problems for dentists and other office personnel, reducing efficiency and effectiveness of a software implementation. Vendors should consider applying user-centered design methodologies to reduce the number of potential usability problem.

DISCUSSION

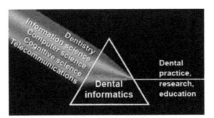

Fig.1. Dental informatics combines its methodological foundations to address problems in practice, research and education.

Dental informatics is a developing body of knowledge that focuses on organization, management and distribution of information in support of dental education, practice, research and administration. It is a subdiscipline of bioinformatics. Friedman has described the tower of science in biomedical informatics. Model formulation, at the lowest level of the tower, is primarily concerned with developing theories and abstractions in the biomedical domain. Such models are representations of the real world and can describe objects, concepts, or methods. Once a model has been formulated, the next step is to develop a computing system that implements the model and allows end users to interact with it. Once a system has been programmed, it must be installed. Evaluation occupies the top level of Friedman's tower. At this level, informaticians conduct formal studies of the effects of implemented systems. Considering the potential outcomes of such systems on the health of individuals, groups, and populations, evaluation is critical.[47]

The most potent force for change in dental practice today and in the future will be dental research. Diagnostic research is growing by leaps and bounds. Techniques for three-dimensional radiography-CAT scans of the mouth, clinical developments in holography, digital subtraction radiography, nuclear medicine techniques, magnetic resonance imaging and developmental biology have been developed. The use of supercomputers to mimic and model oral tissue interactions during health and disease will further expand the area of research.[33]

Research must address issues regarding information architecture, forms of data and information representation, security, privacy, controlled vocabularies, interfaces to other systems, and many other considerations. Computer-based tools for dental research must be developed in accordance with state-of-the-art software engineering principles, so that they can evolve and be re-used by as many researchers as possible. Knowledge management and dissemination are crucial to enhance the efficiency and efficacy of dental research. To standardize the vocabulary, the American Dental Association's Current Dental Terminology (CDT) has been updated and augmented regularly, but is limited to treatment procedures.

Advances in the mainstream of education research, such as adaptive hypermedia, intelligent tutoring systems, simulations, and decision support systems for education need to be applied, evaluated, and validated in biomedical environments.

To help dental informatics augment its ability to accomplish its research goals, the following recommendations may be helpful:

(1) Create a more focused, worldwide community of dental informaticians.

(2) Get more biomedical informaticians interested in dental problems.

(3) Provide career opportunities and career paths for dental informatics researchers.

(4) Address grand challenges together as a community.

(5) Recruit subsequent generations of dental informaticians.[46]

According to Bose, e Learning involves the use of Internet and other related information technologies to create experiences that foster and support the process of education.[12]

The goal of dental education is to teach students a new vocabulary, basic bio-psychosocial sciences, complex procedures, ethics, and professional and business management.

Dental education is faced with a transfer problem. The continuum from basic science to applied science, from normal to abnormal, from molecular to broad human application, and from theoretical to real patients living the theories begs for a bridge between contexts. Interactive patient simulations can address this problem. Software currently available e.g., DDxTx has made it possible to author realistic, effective interactive multimedia patient simulations. These interactive tools provide a realistic context for practice, aid in developing sound information gathering skills, and reinforce concepts from initial learning. Interactive cases simulate the clinical patient but allow students to practice, make mistakes, learn from feedback, and develop problem-solving and decision-making skills. CASE STUDIES FOR dentistry (CSD; MACROMEDIA, San Francisco, CA) is an example of an authoring system for interactive multimedia computer-based patient simulations that would be capable of filing this transfer role for dental students. With this, students collect information, evaluate that information, propose alternate theories based on that information, and make independent decision. Such a tool requires knowledge transfer from initial learning to application and exhibits information like interactivity, random access, anytime/anywhere utilization, decision making and feedback without any testing or penalties.

To date, the most obvious, and most successful, application of computer technology to dental education has been in the dental clinic. Early evidence of a broader interest in educational computing came from Nebraska with the development of 30 dental patient care simulations. In the mid 1980s, The University of Iowa picked up the dental simulation gauntlet, using videodisc technology. In 1988, the American Association of Dental Schools produced a "training" videodisc for dental anatomy. An increased emphasis on the relevance of the basic sciences and more obvious efforts to integrate the basic and clinical dental sciences has been called for. The goal is to learn the skills of problem solving and the acquisition of relevant knowledge in the context in which it is needed. In this information-gathering process, the value of computers, their large clinical databases and their regularly maintained knowledge and image bases is important. Teaching with technology has many wide-ranging positive effects, including facilitation of individualized learning and cooperative learning, as well as institutional partnering.

When designing new methods for teaching the developing professionals potent "patient-driven" factors to be considered are:

a) Increased problem-solving skills with an ever-expanding universe of facts, pharmaceuticals, and regulations,

b) increased communication with medical and dental colleagues,

c) improved communication with the patient,

d) no decrease in the patient's expectations for high quality and constantly   improving technical skills.

In-office computing includes sophisticated office management programs, electronic data interchange for the transmission of insurance forms and payment, cosmetic imaging for projections of dental and facial treatment, in-office milling of crowns and restorations, on-line access to both drug information databases and the medical literature, and the potential for the digital exposure and storage of radiographs.

A grounding in dental informatics, both from the point of information acquisition for problem-solving and proficiency with in-office software applications, data communication, and hardware capabilities are essential. [1]

Many dental informatics application areas utilize knowledge discovery and data mining (KDD)— semiautomatic pattern, association, anomaly, and statistically significant structure discovery in data. It operates at the intersection of artificial intelligence, machine language learning, computer science, engineering, and statistics. The learning methods can be unsupervised or supervised. It is an iterative process with following steps regarding data: collect and store, pre-process, analyze, validate, and implement. Data collection and storage include study design, sampling, merging, and warehousing.

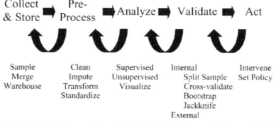

Collect & Store → Pre-Process → Analyze → Validate → Act

Sample	Clean	Supervised	Internal	Intervene
Merge	Impute	Unsupervised	Split Sample	Set Policy
Warehouse	Transform	Visualize	Cross-validate	
	Standardize		Bootstrap	
			Jackknife	
			External	

Fig. 1 — Knowledge discovery and data mining (KDD) steps. KDD involves several iterative steps, beyond analytic algorithms, to process scientific information.

Limitations inherent in study designs remain when Knowledge discovery and data mining is used. However, the methods may provide advantages over traditional statistical methods in dental data.[19]

The acronym **"DICOM"** stands for **digital imaging and communication in medicine** and was first adopted conceptually in the early 1980s by joint activity of the American College of Radiology and the National Electronic Manufactures' Association. It provides a detailed specification for formatting and exchanging images media, including radiographs and photographs used in dentistry. The DICOM standard is broad and the latest version can support the following specialties:

- Intraoral radiography

- Panoramic radiography

- Cephalometric radiography

- Tomography

- Skull and sinus radiography

- CT, ultrasonography, MRI< positron emission tomography, and nuclear medicine

- Intraoral cameras and endoscopy

- Microscopy (surgical and histologic)

- Wave-form representations (e.g, electrocardiogram and electroence-phalogram)

The American Dental Association (ADA) became a member of DICOM Standards Committee in 1996. In 1998, the digital radiograph supplement to the DICOM standard was approved, which applies to transmission radiographs, including those used in dentistry. In 1999, the visible light supplement to the DICOM standard was approved, which applies to video, endoscopic, and microscopic images used in dentistry and the dental specialties.

Radiographic information has developed rapidly in medicine during the past few years. Various systems commercially available are Picture Archiving and Communicating Systems (PACS), Image or Information Archive and Communicating Systems (IMACS).

DICOM incorporates the Open System Interface (OSI) levels, developed by the International Telecommunications Union (ITU) in medical imaging applications, and the Transfer Control Protocol /International Protocol (TCP/IP) developed by the US Department of Defense.

Importance of transmitting dental images are:

1. Referral for second opinions and specialists' advice.
2. To obtain prior approval from treatment from 3rd party insurance carriers and for proof of services rendered prior to reimbursement.
3. Transmission of dental radiographs has value for forensic identification.

Direct digital systems-which use charge –coupled devices (CCD) for intraoral dental radiography are available, Radiovisiography (RVG), the VIXA, Sens-A-Ray, Flash-Dent-record the images in tagged image format file (TIFF)-these systems facilitate teleradiology, offer reduced patient exposure to radiation and a wider range of contrast compared with conventional intraoral radiography.[1]

One of the major reasons for dentistry's reluctance to adopt clinical computer technology to a larger extent is the lack of integration of information technology with the clinical work environment.

Fig.2. Three approaches to software integration.

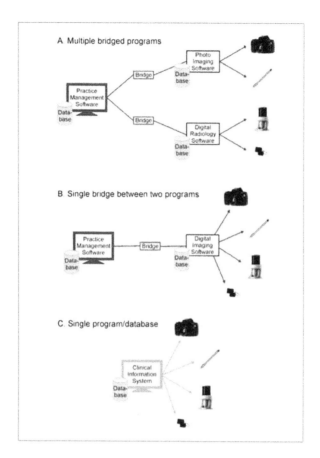

To achieve true integration, hardware, information and software in the dental office should be considered as one system. A second principle in integration is that it should be task-oriented. True integration supports the work flow of the initial examination in a very natural way so that the dentist can concentrate on the actual task, rather than the mechanics of it.(Fig.2)

Four levels of integration

1. Hardware-hardware integration
2. Hardware-software integration.
3. Software integration
4. Task-oriented information integration.

DRI software [PlanmecaOy, Helsinki, Finland]) has been designed which includes a full computer-based oral health record, decision-support functions and modules for collaboration with other dentists and dental technicians. (Fig.3)[49]

Useful integration will occur only with significant investments in research and development by the dental industry as a whole. Integration not only increases efficiency, but also has the potential to improve patient outcomes.[45]

Most of today's speech recognition systems are software-based solutions that are more adaptive than their hardware-based forebears. . Speech recognition engine (SRE) software relies on complex mathematical algorithms to assign to each sound an identifier, which enables the software to distinguish voice sounds from

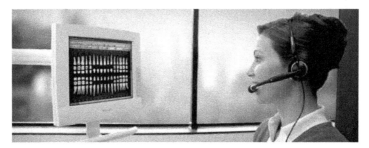

Fig.3 The Dentrix Voice Pro-Hands free charting.

background noise. Context evaluations follow a series of steps, according to Kaprielian: "(1) listen for speech, (2) identify the phonemes [basic units of sound used to distinguish different words], (3) match the phonemes to the words, and (4) make an educated guess as to the context."

Voice-activated systems used in clinical settings are of two types.

- Command-driven voice system
- Dictation system

The different voice-activated software systems available are Dentech, Dentrix, EagleSoft, Easy Dental, Genesis Dental Software, MOGO, PracticeWorks and SoftDent.

Advantages of using voice activation include efficient working with fewer distractions, elimination of redundancy, cost effectiveness and improvement in patient retention and practice image.[14]

VisualDx is a software program that provides assistance in the identification of dental and medical diseases (Fig.4).The Oral Lesions module of VisualDx Version 4.0 is intended to help clinicians identify oral and facial lesions and allows the user to identify a disease by typing the name of the diagnosis or by providing different clinical clues such as lesion type, distribution, and/or findings (Fig.5). The software matches the given clues and generates a list of possible diagnoses. When selecting a diagnosis, the software displays textual information, which includes a synopsis, elements to look for, diagnostic pearls, and differential diagnoses (if applicable), as well as other data. At the same time, images illustrating the diagnosis appear next to the text. In addition, the user can select several diseases simultaneously, for which the software displays respective images side by side, thus enabling a visual differential diagnosis.[56]

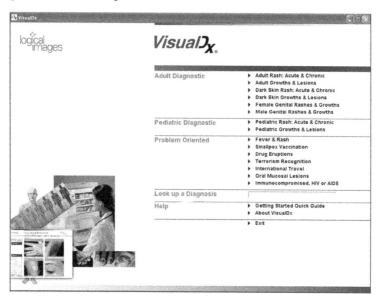

Fig 4. VisualDx's main screen: the screen provides several approaches for users to locate diagnoses.

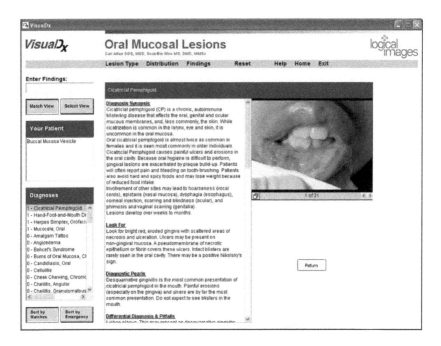

Fig.5. VisualDx's in-depth information for each specific diagnosis via text, while at the same time displaying related clinical images.

Computer-assisted instruction in orthodontics has varied from text-based programs, with or without graphics, concentrating on cephalometrics fundamentals and current clinical procedures to case based expert systems that match a give case to a previously treated case for treatment planning (Fig.6). To prepare the digital records, facial and intra-oral radiographs and photographs can be digitized, and study models in centric occlusion can be photographed digitally. The pre-treatment index page containing links to patient medical record and dental history page, clinical examination form, treatment plan form, extra-oral image, intra-oral images, study model images, and radiographs. Each of the images can be enlarged for better viewing.[28]

Computer analysis of face shape in 3-D can detect subtle differences in face shape and hence support the diagnosis of such congenital abnormalities as Noonan Syndrome. Two- and 3-D models of craniofacial shape, of both soft and hard tissues, can be combined to facilitate the analysis, treatment, and auditing stages.

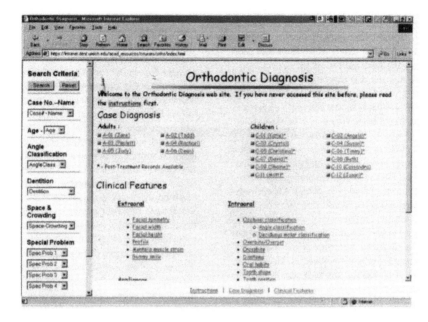

Fig 6. The web site home page contains links to user instruction, case diagnosis, and image archive of clinical features and appliances.

RaPiD, a computer-aided design (CAD) tool enhanced with the knowledge of expert prosthodontists, has been developed to guide dentists to more acceptable designs (Fig 7). With just a few mouse clicks, a clinician can generate a draft design semiautomatically. The Point Distribution Models have been used to determine the variation in dentition in a large number of digitized dental cast images (Fig.8). The semi-automated cephalometric analysis is possible, reducing the time taken to prepare an orthodontic/orthognathic treatment plan (Fig. 9). Models are being developed using three-dimensional photogrammetry to "simulate" soft-tissue change from the pre-surgery hard and soft images and a desired hard-tissue change (Fig.10). This would be used for patient education and to aid in surgery planning. It is useful to be able to discriminate between individuals with a syndrome and controls or between individuals with different syndromes.[22]

The virtual articulator will reduce significantly the limitations of mechanical articulator and, by simulating real patient data, allow analysis of static and dynamic occlusion and gnathic relations and joint conditions. A CAD module is useful in improving the functional occlusion by manipulating the occlusal surface. An orthodontic set-up module allows an individual setup of selected teeth or whole arch. Combining the image data and a virtual set up of suprastructure, an implant –positioning tool

42

would guide a navigation system to the best implant position. To study the impact of joint determinants on occlusal movement patterns, the virtual articulator requires virtual tools for joint-constraint adjustment and collision detection which simulate the stops of static and dynamic occlusion. Such collision detection is implemented in most recent version of the VR articulator has been developed in cooperation with the Fraunhofer Institute for Computer graphics and Kettenbach GmbH & Co KG.[45]

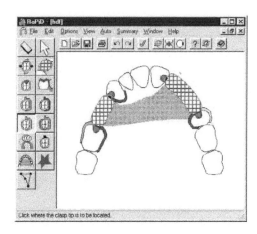

Fig. 7 — Design using RaPiD software.

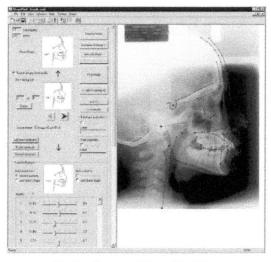

Fig. 8 — Shape modeling of dentition.

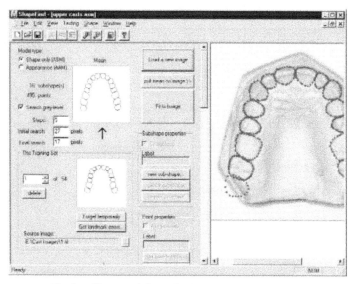

Fig. 9 — Shape modeling using lateral head radiographs.

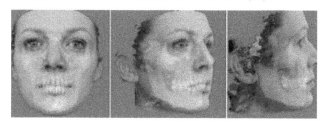

Fig.10. Combination of the i-CAT cone beam scan of the teeth and skeletal structure with the
3dMD face scan that has been co-registered.

Nanotechnology is about manipulating matter, atom by atom. Just as robots assemble cars in factories from a set of predefined parts, nanorobots will assemble things from atomic and molecular building blocks. Nanorobots exert precise control over matter. Nanotechnology will change dentistry, health care and human life more profoundly than many developments of the past. Nanodevices have the potential to bring about significant benefits, such as improved health, better use of natural resources and reduced environmental pollution.[48]

The incorporation of electronic storage of diagnostic information opens up two new opportunities for the practitioner. The first involves the addition of decision-support systems to their current software and the second involves the incorporation of quality assessment measures into their practice management reporting programs. An empty EDPR would be the receptacle for all patient information which includes patient demographics, chief complaint, medical and dental history, extra-oral, oral, periodontal, dental and home care charting, diagnostic tests and results, problem list, diagnoses, treatment plan, treatment record, progress notes, medical or dental laboratory prescriptions, letters of referral or consultation, and a record of patient education, instructions and acceptance of treatment, digitized photographs of the patient and relevant casts, digitized radiographs, and the actual prosthodontic designs ready for transmittal directly to the dental lab.

Data capture may be accomplished by electronic periodontal probes, digital radiographs, voice entry, touch screen, light-pen and graphics tablets.[1]

Among the basic features needed for charting software are the following:

- variable patient look-up by name;
- patient identification number;
- medical health alerts;
- treatment planning and tracking of procedures performed and pending;
- comprehensive display of treatment completed and planned;
- medical history interview and data recording;
- all ADA-approved treatment and diagnostic codes with associated modifiers particular to the specialty being charted.

When the electronic records of the physician, dentist, and other health care professional are dynamically linked, all involved providers will have access to a single electronic health history.[13]

It should be possible to envision a "home base" screen from which any aspect of the patient's record can be accessible with a single click of a button, a voice command, or other means of selection. It should be a large (at least 19"), true-color (24-bit) screen, easily visible to both patient and dentist in every dental operatory in the practice. The final aspect of "display" technology involves the use of color printers which will be able to produce excellent patient education materials such as dental charts or graphs of patient progress, and photographs from the patient's own mouth.

The most obvious impact of the increasing use of an electronic dental patient record in practice will be the value of teaching students how to use such a "chart" while still in school. It could provide students (and practitioners in the form of home-based continuing education) with a clinical window through which they can study the patient "cases" available within their problem-based curriculum materials. The dental office computer system of the future must contain not only the relatively static

45

summary of treatment codes, which has been the cases for many years, but also the shifting oral status, diagnostic, and treatment assessment information. This expanded set of information must now be housed in what has been described previously by this author as a "second generation" or procedural clinical database.

Health care can be improved if a computer system can automatically provide appropriate diagnostic or treatment reminders. Also, it will form the basis for personal quality assurance. With digital charting, all dental team members chart the same way, and the charting shorthand is standardized. Among the basic features needed for charting software are the following: variable patient look-up by name; patient identification number; medical health alerts; treatment planning and tracking of procedures performed and pending; comprehensive display of treatment completed and planned; medical history interview and data recording; all ADA-approved treatment and diagnostic codes with associated modifiers particular to the specialty being charted.[1]

Diagnostic codes are computer-readable descriptors of patients' conditions contained in computerized patient records. The codes uniquely identify the diagnoses or conditions identified at initial or follow-up examinations that are otherwise written in English or French on the patient chart. Dental diagnostic codes would allow dentists to access information on the types and range of conditions they encounter in their practices enhance patient communication, track clinical outcomes and monitor best practices. Different systems of diagnostic codes have been implemented by program managers in Germany, the United Kingdom and North America. In Toronto, the former North York Community Dental Services developed and implemented a system that follows the logic used by the Canadian Dental Association for its procedure codes. The American Dental Association is now preparing for the release of SNODENT codes.

The Toronto system is numeric (4 digits) and was developed for use in the former North York Community Dental Services, a school-based pediatric dental program. The first digit indicates the major category; the second digit indicates the classification of the major condition. The third digit usually indicates whether the primary or the permanent teeth are affected and the last digit specifies the number of teeth affected or the severity of the condition. SNODENT codes are a part of SNOMED, a much larger system of coding medical conditions maintained by the College of American Pathologists. SNODENT is a comprehensive taxonomy that contains codes for identifying not only diseases and diagnoses but also anatomy, conditions, morphology and social factors that may affect health or treatment.

They are alphanumeric with 7 or 8 characters, and are organized according to the etiology of the condition (genetic, infectious, trauma, etc.)[32]

International statistical classification of diseases:

Malignant neoplasms of lip, oral cavity and pharynx **(C00-C14)**

C00 Malignant neoplasm of lip

C01 Malignant neoplasm of base of tongue

C02 Malignant neoplasm of other and unspecified parts of tongue

C03 Malignant neoplasm of gum

C04 Malignant neoplasm of floor of mouth

C05 Malignant neoplasm of palate

C06 Malignant neoplasm of other and unspecified parts of mouth

C07 Malignant neoplasm of parotid gland

C08 Malignant neoplasm of other and unspecified major salivary glands

C09 Malignant neoplasm of tonsil

C10 Malignant neoplasm of oropharynx

C11 Malignant neoplasm of nasopharynx

C12 Malignant neoplasm of pyriform sinus

C13 Malignant neoplasm of hypopharynx

C14 Malignant neoplasm of other and ill-defined sites in the lip, oral cavity and pharynx.

Diseases of oral cavity, salivary glands and jaws (K00-K14)

K00 Disorders of tooth development and eruption

K01 Embedded and impacted teeth

K02 Dental caries

K03 Other diseases of hard tissues of teeth

K04 Disease of pulp and periapical tissues

K05 Gingivitis and periodontal disease

K06 Other disorders of gingival and edentulous alveolar ridge

K07 Dentofacial anomalies (including malocclusion)

K08 Other disorders of teeth and supporting structures

K09 Cysts of oral region, not elsewhere classified

K10 Other diseases of jaws

K11 Diseases of salivary glands

K12 Stomatitis and related lesions

K13 Other diseases of lip and oral mucosa

K14 Diseases of tongue [24]

Well-integrated systems, designed around the work flow of the dental team, can allow care providers to concentrate what they do best: delivering patient care. Such systems provide information when and where it is needed, minimize indirect and duplicative data entry, capture information at the source and are easy to use. Computing applications for dental practice generally are separated into administrative and clinical categories. The administrative and clinical technologies have been grouped into "must-have," "nice-to-have" and "optional" categories. "Must-have" applications are essential to the functioning of a dental practice (such as patient registration, practice reporting and electronic claims submission, which has become more standardized as a result of the Health Insurance Portability and Accountability Act of 1996).

All administrative applications are relatively technologically mature and central to the operation of a dental practice. Clinical applications fall into all three priority categories. Some of them are relatively mature, easy to use and widely applicable, such as software for dental and medical history and treatment planning.

Others—such as progress notes, charting and digital imaging—are technologies approaching relative maturity.

The well-equipped dental office should be designed with IT as a part of the infrastructure, rather than added on as an afterthought (Fig.11).

A monitor for patient viewing is directly integrated into the chair to show the patient intraoral images of his or her mouth for diagnosis and treatment purposes. The dentist and the assistant simply use a specialized mouse or trackball, or their voices, to interact with the computer. A second computer—primarily for use by the dentist, hygienist and dental assistant has a keyboard and is used for a variety of data entry and retrieval purposes, such as treatment planning, scheduling, charting and accessing Internet resources.

An intraoral camera is one of the instruments in the delivery system. Direct digital radiology sensors in different sizes are held by mountings on the chair base. A digital camera is available for extraoral

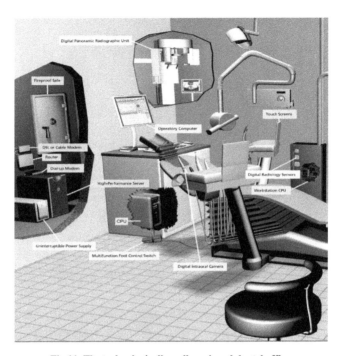

Fig.11. The technologically well-equipped dental office

photographs. In a separate room, a digital panoramic radiographic unit is connected to the practice management system through another computer workstation.

A device that combines the functions of a laser printer, fax machine, scanner and copier is a space-saving and economical way to provide several disparate functions.

A computer is available in the waiting area so that patients can enter their personal registration data and their complete health and dental histories, as well as review dental health information relevant to them.

The nerve center of the practice is the server room. This locked, climate-controlled and secure room contains the server, which all workstations in the practice use to store and retrieve data. Its disk storage should be a redundant array of inexpensive disks, or RAID. A RAID minimizes the probability of a debilitating disk crash.

A digital subscriber line or cable modem provides a high-speed connection to the Internet. Another option for networking computers in the office is a wireless network, Encrypted wireless fidelity, or

WiFi, a new wireless networking standard. Wireless networks afford much greater flexibility in the placement and number of computer workstations. In addition, they open up possibilities for integrating wireless digital cameras, printers, personal digital appliances and similar devices. Issues to be considered in technology purchasing decisions include usability, integration, work flow support, cost-benefit analysis and compliance with standards.[42]

With such a phenomenal potential that dental informatics has in transforming the way dental research, education and clinical practice is carried out, it itself faces challenges. When truly significant scientific challenges are overcome, it profoundly changes the daily activities, as well as the future research activities, of everyone involved in the related field. By identifying and describing the grand challenges facing a scientific field, funding agencies can be helped to identify and prioritize projects for support, stimulate and encourage new investigators to work on these intellectual and technological challenges, and help define the field itself. The challenges described by Sittig et al include:

1. The development of a knowledge-based ontology of dental concepts from which one could extract a standardized controlled clinical terminology to describe dental signs, symptoms, conditions, diseases, and treatments. Such ontology forms the basis of the field of dental informatics.

2. The development of an evidence base of etiology, diagnosis, prevention, treatment, and treatment outcomes (including materials, methods, techniques, and usage) for a large proportion of dental patients and dental practices.

3. To develop a comprehensive electronic oral health record that is seamlessly integrated into the automated medical record.

4. To develop a nationwide oral health database that contains basic patient-level diagnostic, treatment, and outcome data linked to a nationwide medical database.

5. To automate data capture, integration, and synthesis to create real-time, knowledge-based, clinical monitoring systems based on both continuously and intermittently available analog and digital data.

6. To develop learner-centered educational systems that select a learning goal, evaluate the student's abilities, and determine the individual learning style.

New techniques and technologies to help overcome these challenges would facilitate the development of truly monumental applications, such as a comprehensive electronic oral health record, an automated dental treatment planning system for all diagnoses, or a system to profile patient risk for chronic oral diseases.[51]

50

SUMMARY AND CONCLUSION

The application of the science of dental informatics to the various aspects of dentistry –the research, education, basic and clinical sciences-has an unparallel potential for transforming the very face of it.

Upcoming techniques like developmental biology and genomics can unfold many mysteries underlying the disease process and our understanding of these. The computers and the educational software can revolutionize the dental education and help overcome the daunting task of transfer of knowledge from basics to the clinical sciences.

The clinical sciences too can get benefitted from various softwares developed-like shape modeling and photogrammetry in orthodontics, virtual articulator and RaPiD in prosthodontics, Computer aided designing and machining for restorative dentistry, software like VisualDx in oral diagnosis, DICOM in radiology, behavior management in pedodontics and the list can go on.

The clinical practice transforms with the integration of technology into the dental office and makes the workflow smooth. The practice management systems and the clinical decision support systems lend quality to the clinical practice. Teledentistry ensures dental services in the remote and underserved areas. The development of nanaodevices will give a miraculous extension to dentistry.

Overcoming the scientific challenges faced by the field by identifying and prioritizing projects and supporting the future research activities will help define the field itself. It will profoundly change the daily activities and help dental informatics bring a new dawn on the horizons of dentistry!

BIBLIOGRAPHY

1. **Abbey LM, Zimmerman J.** Dental informatics. New York, NY: Springer-Velag 1991.

2. **Abbey LM.** Some comments on the state of dental informatics. J Dent Educ 1991; 55(10): 647-648.

3. **Actis LA, Rhodes ER, Tomaras AP.** Genetic and molecular characterization of a dental pathogen using genome-wide approach.Adv Dent Res 2003; 17:95-99.

4. **Anusavice KJ.** Informatics systems to assess and apply clinical research on dental restorative materials. Adv Dent Res 2003; 17:43-48.

5. **Atkinson JC, Zeller GG, Shah C.** Electronic patient records for dental school clinics: More than paperless systems. J Dent Educ 2002; 66(5):634-642.

6. **Bailit HL.** Health services research. Adv Dent Res 2003; 17:82-85.

7. **Barath VS, Faber F-J, Westland S, Niedermeier W.** Spectrophotometric analysis of all-ceramic materials and their interaction with luting agents and different backgrounds. Adv Dent Res 2003; 17:55-60.

8. **Bartling WC, Schleyer TK, Visweswaran S.** Retrieval and classification of dental research articles. Adv Dent Res 2003; 17:115-120.

9. **Boynton JR, Johnson LA, Nainar H, Hu JC.** Portable digital video instruction in predoctoral education of child behavior management. J Dent Educ 2007; 71(4):545-549.

10. **Chen JW, Hobdell MH, Dunn K, Johnson KA, Zhang J.** Teledentistry and its use in dental education. J Am Dent Assoc 2003; 134:342-346.

11. **Corry AM.** Utilization of library outreach services by dental school alumni, 1988-1998.J Am Dent Assoc 2001; 132:76-82.

12. **Davis R, Wong D.** Conceptualizing and measuring optimal experience of the elearning environment. Decision Sciences Journal of Innovative Education 2007; 5(1).

13. **Delrose DC, Steinberg RW.** The clinical significance of digital patient record. J Am Dent Assoc 2000; 131:57S-60S.

14. **Drevenstedt GL, McDonald JC, Drevenstedt LW.** The role of voice activated technology in today's dental practice. J Am Dent Assoc 2005; 136:157-161.

15. **Eplee H.** Electronic management systems. Eur J Dent Educ 2002; 6(Suppl.3):152-160.

16. **Finkeissen E, Stamm I, Müssig M, Streicher J, Koke U, Helmstetter C, Hassfeld S, Wetter T.** AIDA: Web agents in dental treatment planning.Adv Dent Res 2003; 17:74-76.

17. **Flores-Mir C, Palmer NG, Northcott HC, Huston C, Major PW.** Computer and internet usage by Canadian dentists. J Can Dent Assoc 2006; 72(3):145.

18. **Flores-Mir C, Palmer NG, Northcott HC, Khurshed F, Major PW.** Perceptions and attitudes of Canadian dentists toward digital and electronic technologies. J Can Dent Assoc 2006; 72(3):243.

19. **Gansky SA.** Dental data mining: Potential pitfalls and practical issues. Adv Dent Res 2003; 17:109-114.

20. **Greenes RA.** Decision support at the point of care: Challenges in knowledge representation, management and patient –specific access. Adv Dent Res 2003; 17:69-73.

21. **Gwilliam JR, Cunningham SJ, Hutton T**. Reproducibility of soft tissue landmarks on three-dimensional facial scans.Eur J Orthod 2006; 28:408-415.

22. **Hammond P, Hutton T , Maheswaran S, Modgil S.** Computational models of oral and craniofacial development, growth and repair. Adv Dent Res 2003; 17:61-64.

23. **Hendricson WM, Panagakos F, Eisenberg E, McDonald J, Guest G, Jones P, Johnson L , Cintron L.** Electronic curriculum implementation at North American dental schools. J Dent Educ 2004; 68(10):1041-1057.

24. **International statistical classification of diseases Tenth Revision (ICD-10).**

25. **Johnson LA.** Biomedical informatics training for dental researchers. Adv Dent Res 2004;17:29-33

26. **Kirshner M.** Adaptive hypermedia: A new paradigm for educational software.Adv Dent Res 2003; 17:38-42.

27. **Koch S.** Designing clinically useful systems: Examples from Medicine and Dentistry. Adv Dent Res 2003; 17:65-68.

28. **Komolpis R, Johnson R A.** Web-Based Orthodontic Instruction and Assessment. J Dent Educ 2002; 66(5): 650-658.

29. **Krishnaraju RK, Hart TC, Schleyer TK.** Comparative genomics and structure prediction of dental matrix proteins. Adv Dent Res 2003; 17:100-103.

30. **Kuo WP.** Overview of bioinformatics and its application to oral genomics. Adv Dent Res 2003; 17:89-94.

31. **Lacopino AM.** The influence of "new science" on dental education: Current concepts, trends and models for future. J Dent Educ 2007; 71(4):450-462.

32. **Leake JL.** Diagnostic codes in dentistry-definition, utility and developments to date. J Can Dent Assoc 2002; 68(7):403-6.

33. **Loe H.** Research on oral diseases and its support on dental education and practice. Adv Dent Res 1988; 2:199-203.

34. **McGrath C, Comfort MB, Luo Y, Samaranayke LP, Clark CD.** Application of an interactive computer program to manage a problem-based dental curriculum. J Dent Educ 2006; 70(4):387-397.

35. **Mendonca EA.** Clinical decision support systems: Perspectives in dentistry. J Den Educ 2004; 68(6):589-597.

36. **Oak MR.** A review on barriers to implementing health informatics in developing countries. Journal of Health Informatics in Developing Countries 2007; 2: 115-125.

37. **Pieper K, Klar R, Kessler P.** Use of a microcomputer for recording dental epidemiologic data. Community Dent. Oral Epidemiol.1981; 9: 78-181.

38. **Rekow D.** Informatics challenges in tissue engineering and biomaterials. Adv Dent Res 2003; 17:49-54.

39. **Robinson MA.** Issues and strategies for faculty development in technology and biomedical informatics. Adv Dent Res 2003; 17:34-37.

40. **Rosenberg H, Grad HA, Matear DW.** The effectiveness of computer-aided, self-instructional programs in dental education: A systematic review of the literature. J Dent Educ 2003; 67(5): 524-532.

41. **Schleyer TK, Johnson LA.** Evaluation of educational software. J Dent Educ 2003; 67(11): 1221-1228.

42. **Schleyer TK, Spallek H, Bartling WC, Corby P.** The technologically well-equipped dental office. J Am Dent Assoc 2003;134:30-41

43. **Schleyer TK, Urquidy HT, Straja S.** Validation of an instrument to measure dental students' use of, knowledge about, and attitudes towards computers. J Dent Educ 2001; 65(9):883-891.

44. **Schleyer TK.** Assessing software usability through heuristic evaluation. J Am Dent Assoc 2007; 138:211-218.

45. **Schleyer TK.** Dental informatics. Dent Clin N Am 2002; 46(3).

46. **Schleyer TK.** Dental informatics: A work in progress. Adv Dent Res 2003; 17:9-15.

47. **Schleyer TK.** Dental informatics: An emerging biomedical informatics discipline. Adv Dent Res 2003; 17:4-8.

48. **Schleyer TK.** Nanodentistry: Fact or fiction? Defining nanometer. J Am Dent Assoc 2000; 131:1567-1568.

49. **Schleyer TK.** Why integration is key for dental office technology. J Am Dent Assoc 2004; 135:4-9 S.

50. **Sebastiani P.** Bayesian machine learning and its potential applications to the genomic study of oral oncology. Adv Dent Res 2003; 17:104-108.

51. **Sittig DF, Kirshner M, Maupome G.** Grand challenges in dental informatics. Adv Dent Res 2003; 17:16-19.

52. **Spallek H, Etzel KR, Maher BS.** Dental school applicants' use of website information during the application process. J Dent Educ 2004; 69(12):1359-1367.

53. **Spallek H.** Adaptive hypermedia: A new paradigm for educational software. Adv Dent Res 2003; 17:38-42.

54. **Spohn E, Hardison D.** Consortium on multi-media information technology to enrich dentistry-committed. J Dent Educ 1990; 54(10): 597-598.

55. **Thyvalikakath TP, Schleyer TK, Monaco V.** Heuristic evaluation of clinical functions in four practice management systems. J Am Dent Assoc 2007; 138(2):209-18.

56. **Torres-Urquidy MH, Collins BM.** Visual Dx clinical decision support software. J Dent Educ 2006; 70(8):892-894.

57. **Van Putten MC.** The use of clinical computer workstations as an educational adjunct in prosthodontics.J Prosthod 1995; 4:42-50.

58. **Wastell DG, Lilley JD.** A role for computers in the management of dental education. Medical Education 1988; 22:55-59.

I want morebooks!

Buy your books fast and straightforward online - at one of world's fastest growing online book stores! Environmentally sound due to Print-on-Demand technologies.

Buy your books online at
www.morebooks.shop

Kaufen Sie Ihre Bücher schnell und unkompliziert online – auf einer der am schnellsten wachsenden Buchhandelsplattformen weltweit! Dank Print-On-Demand umwelt- und ressourcenschonend produzi ert.

Bücher schneller online kaufen
www.morebooks.shop

KS OmniScriptum Publishing
Brivibas gatve 197
LV-1039 Riga, Latvia
Telefax:+371 686 204 55

info@omniscriptum.com
www.omniscriptum.com

www.ingramcontent.com/pod-product-compliance
Lightning Source LLC
Chambersburg PA
CBHW051213050326
40689CB00008B/1297